T0381506

THE INEDIBLE BLT

By Bob Jagers

Order this book online at www.trafford.com
or email orders@trafford.com

Most Trafford titles are also available at major online book retailers.

Illustrated by: Meg Barry. Edited by: Beverly Foley.
Cover Design/Artwork by: Meg and Dave Barry.

Print information available on the last page.

We welcome your comments and suggestions.
Please write Bob Jagers atc/o Downs, 10333 Wayne Road, Livonia, MI 48150 or rbjagers@hotmail.com.
To order a copy of THE INEDIBLE BLT, contact Bob Jagers atc/o Downs, 10333 Wayne Road, Livonia, MI 48150

ISBN: 978-1-4120-6115-5 (sc)

Trafford rev. 10/22/2015

www.trafford.com
North America & international
toll-free: 1 888 232 4444 (USA & Canada)
fax: 812 355 4082

Special Thank You:

Pat Mahon, Eileen Power, Bill Smith, Melody Harris, Rick Jagers, Shirley Witgen, Nancy McCoy, Sharon Bussell, Sue Callahan, Elaine Gilbert, Meg Barry, Beverly Foley

CONTENTS

PREFACE

PARENT'S COMMENTS

Six years ago our family was honored to be able to begin to enjoy the company of a charming, knowledgeable and generous senior citizen that came into my children's classroom once a week to share his life experiences with a room full of restless second graders. Little did I know what a lifelong effect his generosity would have on our whole family.

Bob Jagers' stories have been repeated over and over by so many students that he has worked with over the many years he has been a volunteer. The adventures that he has shared have introduced a vast number of exotic places, interesting facts and fascinating events to a continually growing group of youngsters that will never be quite the same again.

Whether it was his slide shows from his latest vacation to the Great Wall of China or the hug in the hallway because the students missed him while he was away on an adventure, his love of living and learning has been a great gift that he has shared with our community. The impact that another caring adult can have on shaping a young mind is immeasurable.

When Bob Jagers asked me to review his latest book, I was honored. He wanted to know how I thought his *"The Inedible BLT"* system could be best used by teachers, parents or other individuals. Although it is difficult to imagine anyone being as good at *"The Inedible BLT,"* I think this easy system could be a handy resource for anyone that is interested in educating today's children. Whether you are a parent, grandparent or teacher, everyone is constantly educating the children that they love. *"The Inedible BLT"* gives anyone, no matter what their formal educational training, a simple method to introduce information to children in an interesting way. Both classroom-educated and home-schooled students can benefit from using this system. Not only with the knowledge that they gain, but also with the thinking and problem-solving skills that they perfect using this system.

I would encourage anyone that reads this book to consider using the *"The Inedible BLT"* learning system to enhance and encourage the learning that all children are challenged to do.

Sharon Bussell

<u>WHAT IS A BLT?</u>

The Hunt for "The Inedible BLTs"

Children are designed to have fun. If given an assignment, most children will find an entertaining, creative way to accomplish the task. When faced with a challenge, children will instinctively search their problem-solving skills and be in a position to think. When you connect fun with learning and problem solving, you have an excellent combination for young students. The concepts presented in this book have been devised to combine all of these features into an easy, learning system that parents and teachers can use with children of all ages to present a vast amount of information in an entertaining manner.

Most adults and many children know that the acronym "BLT" stands for the tasty sandwich made of bacon, lettuce, and tomato. The author of this book has presented this acronym for years to help children begin to think beyond what lies on the surface of even the simplest set of letters. Even though the author's name is Robert, his students know that his friends call him "Bob." When he combined his nickname with his daily lessons, it became a new use for "BLT," **Bob's Lesson Today**.

Although the name of an instructor utilizing this learning system may not be "Bob" or begin with "B," substituting any interesting "B" word such as building block, brain, brainstorm, etc. for "Bob" will still enable the instructor to follow the model in this book and utilize "The Inedible BLT" system.

Building "The Inedible BLT" Concept

If the users of this instructional aid are not named "Bob," they can modify "*The Inedible BLT*" concept by developing an alternate "B" introduction, such as, "building blocks are square."

Basically an "*Inedible BLT*" consists of a subject that would be of interest to students and a system of problem solving that will tell something special about this subject to make it more interesting and memorable.

A quote by John Lubbock illustrates the advantage of the BLT system:
> "*The important thing is not so much that every child should be taught as that every child should be given the wish to learn.*"

A Simple "Inedible BLT" Example

In this introductory example, a learning opportunity arises when a student sees a cardinal and makes a comment about the bird's color. This could be an interesting subject to explore. With a quick search of the Internet or an encyclopedia additional interesting information is discovered. Some interesting information could be that a cardinal eats fruits, seeds and insects. The cardinal also establishes its territory during the spring and the male cardinal sings with a nice musical tone that is often answered by the female cardinal. The cardinal rarely moves from this territory and does not migrate as many other birds do.

Now that you know the student has an interest in this subject, at a later time you can incorporate "*The Inedible BLT*" problem-solving system that relates to the **cardinal**. It is using a definition for each word clue and permitting the students to find the correct word that fits the definition for each part of the puzzle. This creates an interesting challenge for the students. The students solve the equation until every box has a letter. The instructor adds the special information about the subject to complete the story for the students. As a result of this fun activity, there will have been an interesting presentation involving facts about the subject, and a problem was posed that required a solution to be found.

A male Northern Cardinal

Box	Clue 1	action	Clue 2	action	answer
1	CAPE	minus	APE	=	C
2	PAIN	minus	PIN	=	A
3	PEAR	minus	APE	=	R
4	CARD	minus	CAR	=	D
5	PAIN	minus	PAN	=	I
6	NEAR	minus	EAR	=	N
	Another name for space	minus	The plural of "is"	=	
7	AREA	minus	ARE	=	A
8	MALT	minus	MAT	=	L

Here is an example for a way to present the set of clues for box #7 in the subject:

Box #7: "What is another name for a space" [AREA] now minus "The plural of 'is'" [ARE] and that equals [=] the letter "A."

The other boxes are filled with the answer clues for the subject "CARDINAL" without the word-by-word definition clues. The clues can be presented in a random order to generate more interest.

Children learn and remember more from hands-on involvement than from rote memorization. If they are presented with an interesting story to go along with a hands-on activity, the children will retain what they have learned for a longer period of time. Giving a challenge to the children during the learning process will enhance their memory and their willingness to learn.

It is always better to praise than to criticize children. They should be praised for even the slightest, little things they do.

This involvement also improves the self-esteem of the students. Students enjoy a "high five" and often look forward to this little bit of fun while learning.

When presenting "The Inedible BLT," it is very important to remember the age group of the students. A teacher or parent has to present the information at an appropriate level for the children and **be careful not to raise the students to the level of the instructor**. Consider the grade level of the children, and then select words and clues that correspond to that level. The secret to the success of "The Inedible BLT" system is getting the students actively involved.

Have the students draw the squares on the chalkboard. Let the students place the letters in the squares. The whole class participates in solving the equations and all participants receive high fives and praise for their good work. Every little success helps to develop their self-esteem.

If learning can be made interesting, then the students will listen. If learning can also be made fun, then the students will retain what they are hearing and seeing. "The Inedible BLT" system uses this principle to teach the students problem-solving skills while they are playing a game. Now you and your students are ready to begin your hunt for "The Inedible BLT."

BLT is an acronym for "Bob's Lesson Today." What is an acronym? This is a new and unfamiliar word for these students. However, this is a good example for an instructor to introduce a new word to the students that they will most likely remember. Here is a means for the students to remember the word, how the word sounds, and the correct spelling. An explanation of an "acronym" is that it is a word formed from the first letter of each of the successive parts or major parts of a compound term.

Ask the students, "How many of them have eaten at McDonalds?" Naturally, you will find that most hands are raised. Then ask the students, "What kind of things do their parents order?" The answer that you are looking to receive is "Big Mac." Write the word "bigMac" on the board. The next question to present to the students is, "What is the name of the big black bird that says caw?" The appropriate answer is "crow." Add this word to the message on the board to form "bigMaccrow." The next question to present is, "What is the first thing that Jack must be in the rhyme about Jack and the candlestick?" The rhyme is "Jack be nimble, Jack be quick, Jack jump over the candlestick." The answer is Jack must be "nimble." Add this response to the message that you have written on the board to form "bigMaccrownimble." Tell the students that a few parts of the message are not needed. The "Big M" arches need to go back to McDonalds so that other people can get their lunch. After erasing the "bigM" the remaining message reads "accrownimble." Then tell the students that the last three letters are not needed, so remove the "ble." The message on the board now reads "accrownim." Have the students try to pronounce the word on the board and then explain that this is the phonetic pronunciation for the word ACRONYM. Explain to the students that not only is "BLT" the name of the game that they are playing, but that "BLT" can also be an acronym for a bacon, lettuce and tomato sandwich. The students not only know what an acronym is, but will remember how to pronounce it.

When you hunt for *The Inedible BLT*," the students will become involved in the adventure. Have a student come to the board and place the appropriate number of squares on the board. The number of squares coincides with the number of letters in the title of the subject. Choose another student to place the letters into the squares. The letters are usually placed in a random order, however the puzzle has to be solved to determine what letter is to be placed in the square.

Rebus and crossword puzzles, spelling, phonics, and a little ingenuity are used to develop a problem. The instructor states the problem, but the class must solve the problem in order to determine which letter is required in a square. Once the class has solved the problem, the instructor can tell the student-writer where to place the letter. Solving each problem or puzzle results in obtaining a single letter. The instructor must use some ingenuity to create the appropriate level of problem for the students to solve.

What would be your reaction if a child or student said, "I want more BLT's?" Well, this is the reaction that the author of this book has received from his students for many years. An exciting, new, learning strategy has been presented to a new group of children each time "*The Inedible BLT*" is put into practice.

In "*The Inedible BLT*" system, there are three basic forms of puzzles that are used. These puzzles are "strictly spelling," "strictly phonics" and "the use of vowels." An example of a spelling puzzle is "hockey" minus "choke" results in the letter "Y." An example of a phonics puzzle is "for" minus "4" results in three possible answers, "O", "E", and "U." Here are the possibilities: "4" minus "4" = "O," or "four" minus "for" = "U:" fore minus for = "E".

The third puzzle form, "the use of vowels," is the simplest. Select any letter and relate it to its position in the alphabet, with respect to one of the vowels. For example the letter "R" is the middle letter between the 4th and 5th vowels in the alphabet. The letter "R" could also be the 9th letter after the 3rd vowel or the 3rd letter before the last vowel. There are endless ways to create this type of puzzle.

On the next page is an example of a basic spelling puzzle for the subject "**ELEPHANTS**." The puzzle clues are presented in their proper spelling order, however scrambling the clues creates a greater challenge for the students.

EXAMPLE OF A PUZZLE

Clue 1	action	Clue 2	action	answer
BEAD	minus	BAD	=	E
LEAD	minus	ADE	=	L
RACE	minus	CAR	=	E
PANTS	minus	ANTS	=	P
HAIR	minus	AIR	=	H
AMY	minus	MY	=	A
EARN	minus	EAR	=	N
RATE	minus	EAR	=	T
SEAT	minus	TEA	=	S

Many of the subjects you choose may be related to a foreign country. Showing a world map or a globe to the students will help them understand the relationship that the foreign location has to their present country, city or island. This enables the instructor to introduce a bit of geography into the lesson. Similar concepts could also be utilized to relate an historical event to the subject lesson presented to the students to make the learning of history come alive for them. An example could be an eclipse.

The remainder of this book is designed to give the instructor a detailed resource of problems, puzzles and stories to utilize in a home or a classroom setting. The variety of subjects is endless. The small sampling of interesting subjects and puzzles presented in this book are only the stepping-stones to begin the hunt for "The Inedible BLT"!

HOW THE SYSTEM WORKS

One child puts a number of squares on the chalkboard and numbers them. A second child places letters in the numbered squares. The individual letter is obtained by the class solving a problem, which results in a letter. The letter is put into the proper square as indicated by the teacher. The problem solution is arrived at by answering several clues. The teacher can create separate clues for each letter or, if there is a repeat of a letter, he can develop another set of clues for the duplicate letter. For example: The subject POLAR BEAR has 2 A's and 2 R's: nine problems would be used in the first example and 7 clue sets would be used in the second example.

The following pages include illustrations of various BLTs, their puzzles, stories, pictures, and maps.

MAMMALS

MAMMAL FACTS

Mammals are warm-blooded animals that must have air to breathe. Mammals range from the tiny shrew to the enormous blue whale. Humans are also part of the mammal family.

THE STORY OF MINING ELEPHANTS

The elephants is a huge mammal characterized by a long muscular snout and two long, curved tusks. Highly intelligent and strong, elephants are the largest land animals and are among the longest living, with life spans of 60 years or more. Healthy, full-grown elephants have no natural enemies other than humans. They eat grasses, bark, roots, leaves, and fruit.

This example uses both spelling and homophones (phonics).

There are a number of elephants in Africa that are miners. These elephants have been using their tusks to dig a hole into the side of a mountain. This has been going on for many years. This hole now is over 350 feet long, That is longer than a football field. Why are these elephants doing this? They have discovered there is a certain amount of salt in the rocks and dirt. Elephants need salt for survival. They keep digging for new veins of salt.

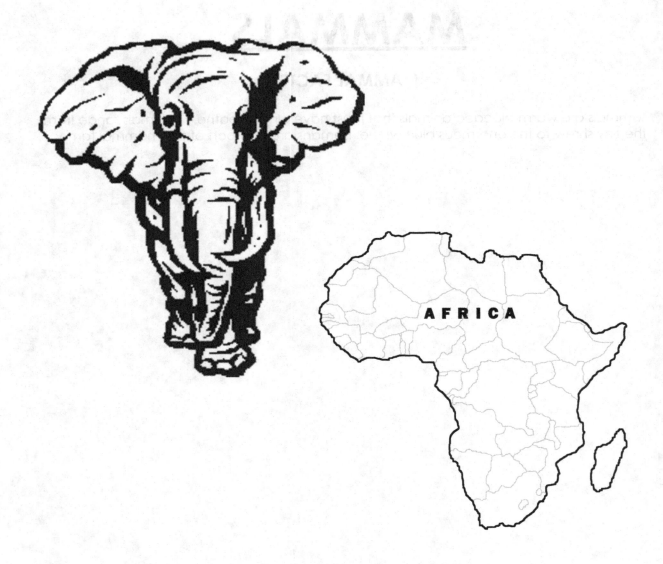

THE ELEPHANTS PUZZLE

Clue 1	Action	Clue 2	Action	Answer
not hard EASY	minus	to speak SAY	=	E
big LARGE	minus	change speeds GEAR	=	L
opposite of love HATE	minus	head wear HAT	=	E
fuzzy fruit PEACH	minus	winner won (one) EACH	=	P
what ears do HEAR	minus	corn carrier EAR	=	H
mom's month MAY	minus	mine MY	=	A
an eraser does CLEAN	minus	to tie shoes LACE	=	N
to carry food TRAY	minus	sunbeam RAY	=	T
place to sit SEAT	minus	past tense of eat ATE	=	S

THE STORY OF THE WALRUS

The walrus has two very long tusks that seem to hang down from its chin. These tusks are used to defend and also used to help the walrus get out of the water. The walrus hooks the tusks onto the ground or ice and pulls itself out of the water.

The master walrus has his own territory and will defend it against any other bull trying to muscle into his harem. The male walrus is called a bull.

THE WALRUS PUZZLE

Clue 1	Action	Clue 2	Action	Answer
room part WALL	minus	everything ALL	=	W
used to measure TAPE	minus	friendly animal PET	=	A
no clouds CLEAR	minus	running event RACE	=	L
rainy month APRIL	minus	water carrier PAIL	=	R
a sheep EWE			=	U
sharp yell SCREAM	minus	goes with ice CREAM	=	S

WALRUS

THE STORY OF THE CAPYBARA

Is it a four-foot long guinea pig? No, its a short-tailed, sleepy-eyed beast known as a capybara — the world's largest rodent. It is found in Venezuela, South America, and some parts of Central America.

The capybara has semi-webbed feet, which helps make it a good swimmer. It spends much of its time around the water or wallowing in the mud with other capybara.

It can weigh as much as 140 pounds (equal to the weight of 2 small students). It is often hunted on horseback. It eats grasses, plants, leaves, etc.

CAPYBARA

VENEZUELA
The capital and largest city is Caracas. Spanish is the official language. The people of Venezuela produce coffee and cocoa, and the country is a main source of crude oil.

THE CAPYBARA PUZZLE

Clue 1	Action	Clue 2	Action	Answer
desert animal CAMEL	minus	cooked dinner MEAL	=	C
necklace part BEAD	minus	place to sleep BED	=	A
dish PLATE	minus	not on time LATE	=	P
letter asks question Y				Y
not sure MAYBE	minus	mom's month MAY	=	B
Illinois STATE	minus	exam TEST	=	A
apple drink CIDER	minus	needed for some games DICE	=	R
hot water STEAM	minus	flower part STEM	=	A

THE STORY OF THE SIFACA MONKEYS

Sifaca monkeys are part of the lemur family of monkeys. This family of monkeys lives on the island of Madagascar. They are on the verge of extinction. There was a Sifaca boy monkey born in the year 2003 at Duke University.

They are long-limbed, and have silky fur. These monkeys walk much like a man, upright. They warn other monkeys of danger by the manner in which they walk.

SIFACA MONKEY

THE SIFACA MONKEY PUZZLE

Clue 1	Action	Clue 2	Action	Answer
too much liquid SPILL	minus	doctors dose PILL	=	S
to catch fish BAIT	minus	night flyer BAT	=	I
chicken FOWL	minus	not high LOW	=	F
oak seed ACORN	minus	we eat the ears CORN	=	A
place to sit CHAIR	minus	covers some heads HAIR	=	C
causes an ouch PAIN	minus	sharp object PIN	=	A

MADAGASCAR
Madagascar lies in the Indian Ocean off the southeast coast of Africa, opposite Mozambique. The world's fourth-largest island, it is twice the size of Arizona.

THE STORY OF THE HIPPOPOTAMUS & THE BARBEL FISH

A hippotumus spends most of the time in the water, but it does not know how to swim. The fish in the same water are not afraid of the hippos, as the large mammals eat the sea-weeds, grasses, and plants. The hippo opens its mouth and the fish swim in and clean out the mouth and the teeth. The hippos have their own private dentists. The only time the hippos eat any meat is when another hippo dies. Then there is a mad scramble for the flesh of the dead hippo. There could be alligators, hyenas, buzzards, or lions vying for the meat of the dead carcass.

A hippo cannot swim but he floats very well. A hippo can stay under water for as long as six minutes. The leader of a group of hippos reigns over his territory. He will be the first one into the water, or the first one to rest. The other hippos will follow.

The lord of the hippos is referred to as the beach master. The beach master must fight other male hippos for control of his territory and over his harem. A harem is a group of females under the leadership of one male.

HIPPOS IN THE WATER

THE HIPPO & FISH PUZZLE

Clue 1	Action	Clue 2	Action	Answer
head covering HEAD	minus	needed for life AIR	=	H
hello HI	minus	aitch H	=	I
smoking tool PIPE	minus	dessert PIE	=	P
mist SPRAY	minus	sunbeams RAYS	=	P
water craft BOAT	minus	baseball wood BAT	=	O
next letter 1, 2, 3, 4, 5, 6		OTTFF	=	S
				&
turn over FLIP	minus	face part LIP	=	F
winter tree PINE	minus	animal cage PEN	=	I
water container GLASS	minus	stays behind LAGS	=	S
to clean WASH	minus	tool with teeth SAW	=	H

THE STORY OF HUMPBACK WHALES

The humpback whale likes to have herring for dinner. Herring move very fast and it is difficult to catch them. The whale likes a lot of herring for dinner because the whale is so large. Whales have developed a system that will force the herring to gather together. The herring are afraid of bubbles. The whale circles the school of herring while blowing bubbles. This causes the herring to get closer and closer. Then at the right time the whale opens its mouth and swallows a large group of herring.

The whale gets its name from the position of the whale after it jumps out of the water. It bends its back to form a humpback. This leaping out of the water is called breeching.

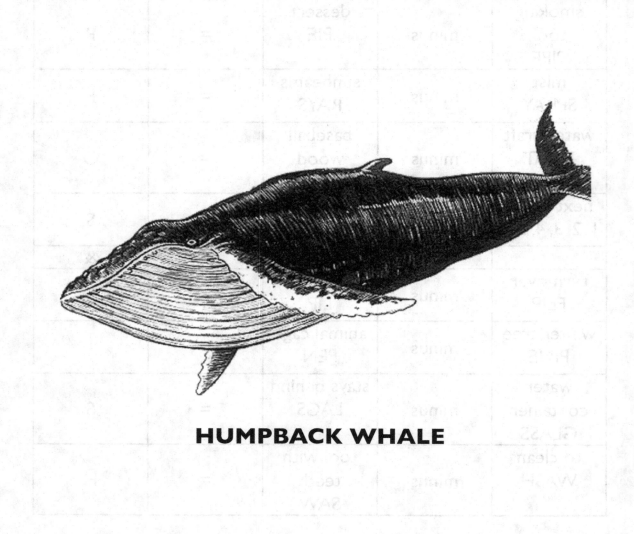

HUMPBACK WHALE

THE HUMPBACK WHALE PUZZLE

Clue 1	Action	Clue 2	Action	Answer
cleaned with a broom SWEPT	minus	stair part STEP	=	W
seaside SHORE	minus	flower ROSE	=	H
not hard EASY	minus	okay YES	=	A
to study LEARN	minus	to merit EARN	=	L
not hard EASY	minus	to speak SAY	=	E
frighten SCARE	minus	contest RACE	=	S

WHALE FACTS
Like other mammals, whales breathe air and are warm-blooded animals. Whales have small eyes, designed to withstand great pressures, and most have good vision. Their hearing is also excellent. Some large whales are believed to have lived 100 years or more in the wild.

THE STORY OF THE NORTH RIGHT WHALES & SEA GULLS

The north right whale lives in the South Atlantic Ocean. The mother whale has to rest and take it easy before giving birth to her baby. She usually comes to the surface and just floats. There is a sea gull that likes to eat the seaweed and other items that cling to the whale's back. Each time a gull pecks at the back of the whale, the mammal has to flick her tail to scare away the gulls. Sometimes, the pecking is so bad that she has to submerge to get rid of the sea gulls. Each time she has to do this she is using more energy. This can cause problems with the baby when it is born. The baby could be sick or even worse it could die. This is the story of a family of whales that could become extinct because of the pesky sea gulls.

NORTH RIGHT WHALE

THE WHALES & GULLS PUZZLE

Clue 1	Action	Clue 2	Action	Answer
letter asks a question **WHY**	minus	greeting **HI**	=	**W**
location question **WHERE**	minus	plural of was **WERE**	=	**H**
to color **PAINT**	minus	1/2 quart **PINT**	=	**A**
why school **LEARN**	minus	to merit **EARN**	=	**L**
bell fruit **PEAR**	minus	musical talk **RAP**	=	**E**
Mississippi has four **S**				**S**
				&
paper leaf **PAGE**	minus	an animal **APE**	=	**G**
W	minus	**U**	=	**U**
not cloudy **CLEAR**	minus	to hurry **RACE**	=	**L**
bottom of a room **FLOOR**	minus	top of a house **ROOF**	=	**L**
winter rain **SNOW**	minus	this moment **NOW**	=	**S**

THE STORY ABOUT POLAR BEARS

Polar bears live in the Arctic region. This area is very cold and it is important for a polar bear to keep dry. The polar bear has a peculiar manner to dry itself after he has been swimming for food. He rubs his fur in the snow. The temperature is so low that the snow is almost dry. He has to do this for his entire body: his head, his paws, his tummy, and his back. If you permit the children to demonstrate this drying procedure, the whole class will remember this event and there will be much laughter. There is another peculiar feature of the polar bear: although its fur is white, its skin is black.

POLAR BEAR

THE POLAR BEAR PUZZLE

Clue 1	Action	Clue 2	Action	Answer
small heap PILE	minus	not true LIE	=	P
4	minus	four	=	O
a light LAMP	minus	road guide MAP	=	L
mom's month MAY	minus	mine MY	=	A
big, black bird CROW	minus	milk machine COW	=	R
TV source CABLE	minus	fancy edge LACE	=	B
VCR need TAPE	minus	soft touch PAT	=	E
change color PAINT	minus	1/2 quart PINT	=	A
a tree fruit PEAR	minus	small veggie PEA	=	R
4th letter after the 4th vowel			=	S

SEA CREATURES

THE STORY OF THE MAGELLAN PENGUINS

The author visited an area that was the natural habitat of the Magellan Penguins. It was difficult to get close to the penguins for a good picture. Therefore, a plan was devised to get close. The penguins would come down a hill and follow a path to the water. One of the daughters traveling with the group would lie down near the top of the hill and when the penguins passed she would rise and make a noise. The penguins would be frightened and try to run down the hill. They would flop onto their bellies and would flap their flippers. It surely was a comical situation. The persons with the cameras would be waiting at the bottom of the hill. Some excellent pictures were taken. It was estimated that there were about 25,000 penguins in this area of southern Argentina. The penguins were always talking. There was a line that was over a mile long. There would be four or five penguins abreast in the line. They were prancing and dancing in this line. The line went all the way to the sea. The penguins at the front of the line would jump into the water and frolic and have fun with other penguins. They would eat some fish and get out of the water and head back to their mate. The male would transfer the food to the mother's mouth and she would give it to the baby. The male would get back into the line and start all over again. The vacationers spent the night in a lighthouse. The penguins made so much noise that we could not sleep.

MAGELLAN PENGUINS

SOUTH
AMERICA

THE PENGUINS PUZZLE

Clue 1	Action	Clue 2	Action	Answer
hold tight CLAMP	minus	seafood CLAM	=	P
to eat DINE	minus	loud noise DIN	=	E
a ring BAND	minus	not good BAD	=	N
rye GRAIN	minus	needed for flowers RAIN	=	G
female relative AUNT	minus	insect ANT	=	U
sand carrier PAIL	minus	lose when you stand LAP		I
pleasant NICE	minus	coldest water ICE	=	N
place to sit SEAT	minus	hot drink TEA	=	S

THE STORY OF THE RED CRABS

There is an island in the Pacific Ocean that is called Christmas Island. This island has millions of red crabs. These red crabs could become extinct because of some yellow ants. How they arrived at Christmas Island is unknown. It is suspected that these undesirable insects came to Christmas Island from Africa. The female crab has a sac on her bottom that can hold over a thousand eggs. She goes from the mating area towards the sea with her eggs. She flaps her sac at the water's edge to place the eggs into the water. Then she starts to go back to the forest and the mating area. The ants get into the nose, eyes, and mouth of the crabs. The ants bite and chew these vital parts of the crabs and the crabs eventually die. There has been a large decrease in the red crab population on Christmas Island over the last few years as the result of these yellow ants.

RED CRABS OF CHRISTMAS ISLAND

THE RED CRABS PUZZLE

Clue 1	Action	Clue 2	Action	Answer
do to a book READ	minus	summer drink ADE	=	R
frighten SCARE	minus	mark after a cut SCAR	=	E
one driving DRIVER	minus	flowing water RIVER	=	D
ocean SEA			=	C
write clearly PRINT	minus	1/2 quart PINT	=	R
place to sit CHAIR	minus	have much money RICH	=	A
place to eat TABLE	minus	not on time LATE	=	B
large department store SEARS	minus	R R R ARES	=	S

BIRDS AND
FLYING CREATURES

THE STORY ABOUT THE CORMORANT BIRDS

The cormorant bird is a bird that obtains its food by fishing. It dives into the water and catches a fish in its mouth. The bird then swallows the fish. The Chinese have found a method of using this bird to do the fishing for the boatman. The Chinese fisherman ties a cord around the bird's throat. This prevents the bird from swallowing the fish. The cormorant catches the fish and comes to the surface and deposits the fish in the boat.

THE CORMORANT PUZZLE

Clue 1	Action	Clue 2	Action	Answer
remove CANCEL	minus	not dirty CLEAN	=	C
promise OATH	minus	covers the head HAT	=	O
needed for a sandwich BREAD	minus	necklace part BEAD	=	R
race distance MILE	minus	untruth LIE	=	M
to permit ALLOW	minus	room part WALL	=	O
to stop BRAKE	minus	to make a cake BAKE	=	R
boat with a paddle CANOE	minus	one time ONCE	=	A
small cut SNIP	minus	small taste SIP	=	N
to sample TASTE	minus	iced drinks TEAS	=	T

CORMORANT BIRD

FISHERMEN ON THE LI RIVER

THE STORY OF CHINESE DUCKS

The Chinese people do not use watchdogs to warn them of people coming into their property. They use ducks. A few ducks in the yard can make a lot of noise when a stranger approaches. The quacking alarms the people inside that strangers are coming. The ducks may even try to bite the strangers.

Divide the class into two groups (maybe boys and girls). Pick a duck leader and explain the difference between friendly people and unknown people. Enter the classroom being a friend or a non-friend and let the children demonstrate the action of the ducks and the whole class will laugh.

CHINESE DUCK

THE CHINESE DUCKS PUZZLE

Clue 1	Action	Clue 2	Action	Answer
3rd vowel	minus	5th letter	=	D
4th vowel	plus	6th letter	=	U
2nd vowel	minus	2nd letter	=	C
4th vowel	minus	4th letter	=	K
4th vowel	plus	4th letter	=	S

China

THE STORY OF THE CURLEW BIRD

The curlew is a shore bird that has a long curved bill. She uses the bill to dig in the sand for her food. She eats worms, insects, and vegetable matter.

There is a species that lives in the Arctic but migrates to Central America. They travel along the east coast of the United States during their migration time.

The curlew does something odd before she eats her dinner. She goes to the nearest water and washes the sand or dirt off her food before she will eat it.

This is a lesson for all of us. We should wash our hands before eating.

CURLEW BIRD

THE CURLEW BIRD PUZZLE

Clue 1	Action	Clue 2	Action	Answer
an ocean SEA			=	C
a winter tree YEW			=	U
driving the car DRIVER	minus	special swimmer DIVER	=	R
blue skies CLEAR	minus	to hurry RACE	=	L
ready to eat RIPE	minus	to tear RIP	=	E
U	plus	U	=	W

THE STORY OF THE HAMERKOP STORK

This bird lives in the marshy areas of Africa and it makes large nests about five feet high and very strong. These nests are covered with snake skins. The nests are sufficiently strong to support the weight of a man. The Hamerkop sometimes will build three or four nests. Other birds or animals occupy the unused nests. The unique feature of this African bird is that it predicts the weather and warns other creatures of the forest that a storm is coming. It does this by the manner in which it sings. It eats tadpoles and frogs. The nest is made from reeds, grasses, and sticks. The hamerkop stork is the size of a heron.

HAMERKOP STORK

THE HAMERKOP STORK PUZZLE

Clue 1	Action	Clue 2	Action	Answer
aitch AITCH			=	H
an oak seed ACORN	minus	we eat the ears CORN	=	A
top of milk CREAM	minus	running contest RACE	=	M
sugar tree MAPLE	minus	light source LAMP	=	E
purple fruit GRAPE	minus	part of a newspaper PAGE	=	R
to gather leaves RAKE	minus	corn measure EAR	=	K
by one's self ALONE	minus	path in the woods LANE	=	O
fruit needing a shave PEACH	minus	won (one) EACH	=	P

THE STORY OF HUMMINGBIRDS

A hummingbird can fly as fast as 45 miles per hour. Their wings beat at the rate of 75 beats per second. They are the only bird that can hover. This means that they can fly in the same space without moving. A hummingbird hovers while it gathers the nectar from the flowers.

There are 300 varieties of hummingbirds. Most hummingbirds weigh three or four grams. A nickel weighs five grams.

The birds flit from flower to flower. They move the nectar from one flower to another. This is called pollination. Pollination is the carrying of pollen to the female part of a plant to fertilize the seed.

HUMMINGBIRD

THE HUMMINGBIRD PUZZLE

Clue 1	Action	Clue 2	Action	Answer
along the water SHORE	minus	achy feeling SORE	=	H
W	minus	YOU	=	U
hold tight CLAMP	minus	applause CLAP	=	M
group of players TEAM	minus	hot drink TEA	=	M
Indian head CHIEF	minus	kitchen head CHEF	=	I
picnic pests ANTS	minus	entered a chair SAT	=	N
person with a halo ANGEL	minus	country path LANE	=	G
not sure MAYBE	minus	mom's month MAY	=	B
to lift RAISE	minus	we have 2 EARS	=	I
daily task CHORE	minus	mountain sound ECHO	=	R
pickle type DILL	minus	not well ILL	=	D

THE STORY OF THE JACANA BIRD

(PRONOUNCED SHASANA)

Pheasant-tailed Jacana is found in China, Africa, India, Australia, and the Philippines. It grows a long tail during breeding. It has long legs, toes and claws. The long and wide spread of its toes permits it to walk on the leaves of lily pads and other plant leaves. This bird is a purplish brown color.

The female mates with several males. She is brighter and bigger than the male. Normally, in most species, the male bird is the larger and has more color. The male has to take care of the nest and raise the babies.

JACANA BIRD

THE JACANA BIRD PUZZLE

Clue 1	Action	Clue 2	Action	Answer
alligator part JAWS	minus	tool with teeth SAW	=	J
many links CHAIN	minus	face part CHIN	=	A
one time ONCE	minus	1st in a race WON (ONE)	=	C
wheat GRAIN	minus	small smile GRIN	=	A
pleasant NICE	minus	coldest water ICE	=	N
do to a book READ	minus	primary color RED	=	A

THE STORY OF THE PHALAROPE BIRD

The phalarope is a water bird that has a problem getting its dinner. This bird cannot dive like most water birds. She has to find a way to bring the food to the surface so she can easily reach it. She flaps her wings and moves her feet, which causes her to spin in the water. She makes a little whirlpool and the small items of food in the water come to the surface. Then at the proper moment she bends over and has her dinner.

This can be demonstrated with a bowl of water and some rice. Place the rice in the water then take a spoon and stir the water. An eddy will be formed and the rice will begin to rise to the surface.

PHALAROPE BIRD

THE PHALAROPE BIRD PUZZLE

Clue 1	Action	Clue 2	Action	Answer
two alike PAIR	minus	needed to live AIR	=	P
not expensive CHEAP	minus	measured step PACE	=	H
Charles NAME	minus	adult boys MEN	=	A
small cut SLIT	minus	enter a chair SIT	=	L
necklace part BEAD	minus	to go at night BED	=	A
group of soldiers ARMY	minus	mom's month MAY	=	R
holds a boat ANCHOR	minus	place for horses RANCH	=	O
red fruit GRAPE	minus	needed to change speed GEAR	=	P
furry animal BEAR	minus	metal rod BAR	=	E

STORY OF THE PITOHUI BIRD

Several years ago a man was studying different birds and he picked up a hooded Pitohui bird. He put his fingers in his mouth and his mouth became very numb. I guess this man thought that he was a baby again. Further examination of this bird revealed that there was a poison in his wing tips. This poison is similar to that found in the poisonous dart frog. The Pitohui bird is orange and black and lives in New Guinea. It is about the size of a pigeon. Researchers believe that the poison comes from a beetle that the bird eats.

THE PITOHUI BIRD PUZZLE

Clue 1	Action	Clue 2	Action	Answer
fall fruit APPLE	minus	type of jump LEAP	=	P
to lift RAISE	minus	corn units EARS	=	I
valentine HEART	minus	ears do HEAR	=	T
permit ALLOW	minus	room part WALL	=	O
after someone CHASE	minus	computer holder CASE	=	H
W	minus	sheep EWE (U)	=	U
water carrier PAIL	minus	friend PAL	=	I

THE BIRD CHOIR STORY

The Kokako bird is a very colorful bird in blue-gray with a wattle. The wattle is like a protection for a baseball catcher's throat, that leather piece that hangs down. It lives only on the islands of New Zealand. It does very little flying, but runs around in the forest. However, in the morning it flies to a treetop and starts singing, before long many other Kokako birds are joining in the singing. Thus, the title of this particular BLT is "The Bird Choir."

THE BIRD CHOIR PUZZLE

Clue 1	Action	Clue 2	Action	Answer
breakfast dish BOWL	minus	not high LOW	=	B
holds food DISHES	minus	storage places SHEDS	=	I
place to eat DINER	minus	special eating DINE	=	R
evergreen CEDAR	minus	running event RACE	=	D
December temperature COLD	minus	grandpa is OLD	=	C
cut wood CHOP	minus	policeman COP	=	H
W	minus	2 sheep EWE-EWE (U-U)	=	O
3 __ men WISE	minus	so SEW	=	I
holds hand ARM	minus	mom MA	=	R

THE STORY OF THE PURPLE STREAK BUTTERFLY

The purple streak butterfly is found in Brazil. The wings of this butterfly change color as the light strikes the brilliant blue color. The wings of this butterfly are often made into jewelry. It is of the morph class of butterflies. There are so many of these butterflies that it does not seem that they could become extinct.

THE PURPLE STREAK BUTTERFLY PUZZLE

Clue 1	Action	Clue 2	Action	Answer
cleaning tool BROOM	minus	part of a house ROOM	=	B
not sure ABOUT	minus	water craft BOAT	=	U
red veggie BEET	minus	honey maker BEE	=	T
to lose weight DIET	minus	to lose life DIE	=	T
book leaf PAGE	minus	space GAP	=	E
eye water TEAR	minus	take food EAT	=	R
turn over FLIP	minus	face part LIP	=	F
why at school LEARN	minus	to merit EARN	=	L
ice game HOCKEY	minus	to gag CHOKE	=	Y

BUTTERFLY

SOUTH AMERICA

THE STORY OF BATS

Bats are important for the growing of fruit trees. They eat the ripe fruit and drop parts of this fruit on the ground to cause pollination. Pollination is the transfer of pollen from flower to flower or tree to tree. This transfer of pollen is necessary for things to grow. The bats are also important from another standpoint. They consume many insects. A bat has built-in radar and can find the insects in the dark. Mosquitoes are a favorite meal for bats. The reason the bats have a web from head to toe is this web acts as a net. A bat catches its prey in the web, then it is easy for the bat to have its dinner.

THE BATS PUZZLE

Clue 1	Action	Clue 2	Action	Answer
need to think BRAIN	minus	need for flowers RAIN	=	B
oak seed ACORN	minus	we eat the ears CORN	=	A
inside pump HEART	minus	ears do HEAR	=	T
sky object STAR	minus	black goo TAR	=	S

BAT

THE STORY ABOUT A BEELINE

The term beeline comes from the fact that after some bees find an acceptable flower for the nectar, they immediately fly in a straight line back to their hive. They then tell other bees where these flowers are. Pollen clings to the bee's feet and is carried from flower to flower. The mixing of the pollen is termed pollination. This is what makes new flowers.

HONEY BEE

THE BEELINE PUZZLE

Clue 1	Action	Clue 2	Action	Answer
place to eat TABLE	minus	not on time LATE	=	B
woods animals BEAR	minus	place for drinks BAR	=	E
breakfast food CEREAL	minus	not cloudy CLEAR	=	E
shower month APRIL	minus	two alike PAIR	=	L
to lift RAISE	minus	we have two EARS	=	I
not dirty CLEAN	minus	tie shoes LACE	=	N
where ushers work AISLE	minus	catches the wind SAIL	=	E

<u>PEOPLE</u>

THE STORY OF GEORGE WASHINGTON CARVER

Ask the students, "How many like peanut butter?" Most of the children will raise their hands. You inform them that a former slave discovered peanut butter. This slave did not know his name and was orphaned when he was young. Moses and Susan Carver raised him on their farm. They gave him the name of George Washington Carver.

George was born in Missouri and later went to college in Iowa. He studied science and agriculture (farming) and later taught at the Tuskewgee University in Alabama. He became head of the Agriculture Department and taught there for over 50 years. He gave his savings to a special fund to be used for agriculture research.

George Washington Carver developed hundreds of products from peanuts, sweet potatoes, pecans, and soy beans. His discoveries greatly improved the farmers' products in the south. The principal crop in the south before Mr. Carver was cottton. He invented a substitute for rubber. He developed some adhesives, dyes and many other products.

He died in 1943.

GEORGE WASHINGTON CARVER

This story illustrates the fact that no matter how poor is one's background, you can make a name for yourself.

THE GEORGE WASHINGTON CARVER PUZZLE

Clue 1	Action	Clue 2	Action	Answer
Jim GYM	minus	my MINE	=	G
Superman's cloak CAPE	minus	bottle top CAP	=	E
not after BEFORE	minus	B4	=	O
do to a book READ	minus	summer drink ADE	=	R
rye or oat GRAIN	minus	needed for flowers RAIN	=	G
box for breakfast CEREAL	minus	no clouds CLEAR	=	E
2 sheep EWE-EWE			=	W

MISSOURI

Jefferson City

Clue 1	Action	Clue 2	Action	Answer
animal with a hump CAMEL	minus	boy or man MALE	=	C
space AREA	minus	corn measure EAR	=	A
to whittle CARVE	minus	hole in mountain CAVE	=	R
take a trip TRAVEL	minus	not now LATER	=	V
"TLC" CARE	minus	something in the garage CAR	=	E
apple drink CIDER	minus	needed for some games DICE	=	R

THE STORY OF ASSASSINATED PRESIDENTS

There were four presidents who were killed during their time in office. Abraham Lincoln was shot while attending a theater performance in Washington, D.C. James Garfield was shot while greeting people in a Washington, D.C., railroad station. William McKinley was shot in the Temple of Music in Buffalo, New York. John F. Kennedy was shot while riding in a convertible automobile in Dallas, Texas. They were the 16th, 20th, 25th, and 35th presidents.

A riddle comes to mind while the children are trying to answer the puzzle. Name two presidents who are not buried in the United States. Answer: Any two past presidents still living.

LINCOLN
16th President

GARFIELD
20th President

McKINLEY
25th President

KENNEDY
35th President

THE PRESIDENTS PUZZLE

Clue 1	Action	Clue 2	Action	Answer
1/8 of gallon PINT	minus	soft metal TIN	=	P
person steering DRIVER	minus	special swimmer DIVER	=	R
place to sit SEAT	minus	past tense of sit SAT	=	E
area SPACE	minus	a step PACE	=	S
water carrier PAIL	minus	lose when you stand LAP	=	I
finished DONE	minus	winner WON (ONE)	=	D
not alive DEAD	minus	mom's mate DAD	=	E
places for horses RANGES	minus	change speeds GEARS	=	N
need a drink THIRST	minus	something to wear SHIRT	=	T
price COST	minus	camp bed COT	=	S

EVENTS AND SPECIAL DAYS

THE STORY OF HALLOWEEN

The word Halloween comes from two words: hallowed and evening. Hallowed means holy and the poetic word for evening is een. Halloween comes on October 31. This is the day before All Saints Day. The saints were the holy ones in the Catholic Church. The 31st of October is the evening before November 1st, which is All Saints Day.

THE HALLOWEEN PUZZLE

Clue 1	Action	Clue 2	Action	Answer
water's edge SHORE	minus	a flower ROSE	=	H
beauty and the ___ BEAST	minus	tops BEST	=	A
storage place CELLAR	minus	blue skies CLEAR	=	L
place to eat TABLE	minus	tempo BEAT	=	L
water vessel BOAT	minus	night flyer BAT	=	O
result of hard play SWEAT	minus	place to sit SEAT	=	W
ready to eat RIPE	minus	to tear RIP	=	E
thin coin DIME	minus	not bright DIM	=	E
walking aid CANE	minus	high card ACE	=	N

THE STORY OF THE MEMORIAL DAY

Henry Welles from Waterloo, New York, suggested a special day to honor the dead from the Civil War. The day he selected was May 5, 1865. However, in May 1868, General John Logan, the 1st commander of the Grand Army of the Republic, gathered a number of local people to lay wreaths and flowers on the graves of the fallen soldiers in their local cemeteries. This became the official beginning of Memorial Day. It was named Decorations Day and later the date was set for May 30. The city of Waterloo, New York, was officially declared as the origin of Memorial Day in 1966.

Memorial Day is celebrated to honor all of the men and women who served in the military. It could be Air Force, Army, Marines, Navy, or Coast Guard. The special feature of this day is to honor all those who gave their lives while serving in the military forces. Many towns and cities celebrate this day with a parade. The author has participated in many Farmington/Farmington Hills, Michigan, parades. He has also participated in other Michigan parades in Muskegon, Redford, and Novi, as well as in New Orleans, Louisiana.

THE MEMORIAL DAY PUZZLE

Clue 1	Action	Clue 2	Action	Answer
top of milk CREAM	minus	running event RACE	=	M
morning food CEREAL	minus	see thru glass CLEAR	=	E
express-way RAMP	minus	talking music RAP	=	M
by one's self ALONE	minus	meat with less fat LEAN	=	O
cleaning tool BROOM	minus	loud noise BOOM	=	R
usher area AISLE	minus	closed deal SALE	=	I
oat or rice GRAIN	minus	small smile GRIN	=	A
under house CELLAR	minus	no clouds CLEAR	=	L

Clue 1	Action	Clue 2	Action	Answer
place for a car ROAD	minus	boat need OAR	=	D
many links CHAIN	minus	face part CHIN	=	A
ice sport HOCKEY	minus	to gag CHOKE	=	Y

ST. PATRICK'S DAY STORY

St. Patrick was born in Wales in 385. He was sold into slavery at the age of 16. He later escaped from slavery and went to various Catholic schools. He went to Ireland and established many schools, churches, and monasteries. He became the patron saint of Ireland. He died on March 17, 461.

The special day of St. Patrick was not celebrated in the United States until 1737, where it was first celebrated in the city of Boston.

You could ask the class to name items that are green; this game could be boys versus girls for an example.

THE ST. PATRICK'S DAY PUZZLE

Clue 1	Action	Clue 2	Action	Answer
not large SMALL	minus	place to shop MALL	=	S
inside pump HEART	minus	ears do HEAR	=	T
covers the floor CARPET	minus	small amount TRACE	=	P
they make oaks ACORNS	minus	we eat the ears CORN	=	A
wood box CRATE	minus	speed contest RACE	=	T
black bird CROW	minus	milk machine COW	=	R
say good things PRAISE	minus	bell fruit PEARS	=	I
erase CANCEL	minus	eraser does CLEAN	=	C
shoe cleat SPIKE	minus	desserts PIES	=	K
places to sit SEATS	minus	one place to sit SEAT	=	S

NATURAL OCCURANCES

THE STORY OF FIRE

The author served in the Navy during World War II. He attended a fire-fighting class. It was during this class that he nearly suffered severe burns. However, the quick thinking and action of the instructor prevented him from this mishap.

The instructors were demonstrating the method of extinguishing a gasoline fire in a room similar to a room on board a ship. This procedure required two men. The first man would enter the room with a high-pressure hose that produced a fine mist. The second man was to protect the first man by spraying him from the second hose. The author was the first man and he entered the room with his hose held high. There was a flash and the second man was frightened and backed away. Fortunately the instructor saw what was happening and immediately grabbed the second man's hose and sprayed the author. If this procedure is not followed according to the instructions a serious explosion could happen.

Most firemen have a saying that helps them remember a very important factor about fires. The saying is "HOUSE ON FIRE" there are three items needed for a fire to burn: heat (house), oxygen (on), and fuel (fire). If any one of these essential items is missing the fire will stop burning.

THE FIRE PUZZLE

Clue 1	Action	Clue 2	Action	Answer
third season FALL	minus	everything ALL	=	F
to catch fish BAIT	minus	night flyer BAT	=	I
rain month APRIL	minus	water carrier PAIL	=	R
morning food CEREAL	minus	no clouds CLEAR	=	E

THE STORY OF TALKING ICE

Glaciers are formed when snow and water fall in a chasm between two mountains. The falling of this combination creates a tremendous pressure on the snow and ice at the bottom of the chasm. This buildup of pressure causes the ice at the bottom to move downward. This movement along the bottom and along the mountain's sides creates many weird noises: groaning, grinding, ice sliding along ice. It appears that the ice and snow are talking to each other. The faster-moving ice in the center is telling the slower moving ice that is along the sides of the mountain, "to move faster or get out of the way." The ice in a glacier is a bright blue. The force behind the front of a glacier is so strong that it often forces the front part of the glacier to break off.

THE TALKING ICE PUZZLE

Clue 1	Action	Clue 2	Action	Answer
body pump HEART	minus	ears do HEAR	=	T
baby's pants DIAPER	minus	feel something good PRIDE	=	A
knife part BLADE	minus	a drop of sweat BEAD	=	L
nice dessert CAKE	minus	high card ACE	=	K
to lift RAISE	minus	hearing tools EARS	=	I
at no time NEVER	minus	at all times EVER	=	N
loud noise BANG	minus	to forbid BAN	=	G
two alike PAIR	minus	talking music RAP	=	I
large bird CROW	minus	to move a boat ROW	=	C
alike SAME	minus	our uncle SAM	=	E

GLACIERS

The glacier that the author visited was in Argentina near the border of Chile (South America). The year before his visit the entire front of the glacier broke off. This front was about 200 feet high and about three miles long. There was so much ice that it stopped the flow of the river. The water rose about 15 feet and everything below the water line was killed from the extremely cold water. The portions of ice that break off normally fall into the river. Many weird shapes are formed as the moving river water contacts those pieces of ice from the glacier.

THE GLACIER PUZZLE

Clue 1	Action	Clue 2	Action	Answer
bicycle part GEAR	minus	sound collector EAR	=	G
fancy edge LACE	minus	high card ACE	=	L
coffee seed BEAN	minus	founding father Frankin BEN	=	A
ties shoes LACES	minus	money deal SALE	=	C
2nd vowel	plus	next 4th letter	=	I
no clothes BARE	minus	metal rod BAR	=	E
eraser does CLEAR	minus	fancy edge LACE	=	R

This is a story about the same subject, but with two different titles: "Talking Ice" and "Glaciers." The "Talking Ice" subject title makes it more interesting to the children.

PLACES OF INTEREST

THE STORY OF THE GREAT WALL OF CHINA

The Great Wall of China was built over 2000 years ago and is over 3000 miles in length. It is the only man-made object that can be seen from the moon. It twists and turns over northern China. It is wide enough for five horses abreast. There are some areas of this wall that are very steep. You need to hang onto the railing to go up or down in these areas.

THE GREAT WALL OF CHINA PUZZLE

Clue 1	Action	Clue 2	Action	Answer
book sheet PAGE	minus	small veggie PEA	=	G
green fruit GRAPE	minus	newspaper part PAGE	=	R
not hard EASY	minus	to speak SAY	=	E
oat or rye GRAIN	minus	small smile GRIN	=	A
tempo BEAT	minus	16th president ABE	=	T
sheep EWE	plus	YOU	=	W
water carrier PAIL	minus	mouth part LIP	=	A
a little fat PLUMP	minus	way to move water PUMP	=	L
not small LARGE	minus	anger RAGE	=	L

GREAT WALL OF CHINA

China

MAYAN TEMPLE STORY

The Mayan temple of Kulculkan is located near Merida, Mexico. This temple has some unusual features. It is 4 sided with 91 steps on each side (4 x 91 = 364 + main platform = 365, which is the number of days in a year). This pyramid was used as a calendar for the local people. Each side represented a season. A priest or a helper would place a branch or a plant or a flower on a step. A person could tell what day it was by the pattern between the steps and the particular step on which the subject was placed.

If you were to stand in an exact location at the base of this temple and clap your hands, you could hear the sound travel up the steps and the repeat sound come back down the steps. If you move two feet away from this exact spot and you clap your hands then nothing happens. Modern sound engineers have not been able to understand why this unique feature works.

There is another temple inside of the big temple. There is a jaguar statue inside the inner temple. This jaguar has spots made of jade. The unusual nature of this is that there are no known deposits of jade in Mexico.

TEMPLE OF KULCULKAN

THE MAYA TEMPLE PUZZLE

Clue 1	Action	Clue 2	Action	Answer
hold tight CLAMP	minus	applause CLAP	=	M
a VCR need TAPE	minus	a canary PET	=	A
star flower DAISY	minus	spoken SAID	=	Y
Indian boat CANOE	minus	at one time ONCE	=	A
at no time NEVER	minus	at all times EVER	=	N
need water THIRST	minus	something to wear SHIRT	=	T
cigar ends ASHES	minus	wide belt SASH	=	E
car need MOTOR	minus	tree support ROOT	=	M
fall fruit APPLE	minus	jump across LEAP	=	P
open flower BLOOM	minus	loud noise BOOM	=	L
no clothes BARE	minus	metal rod BAR	=	E

THE STORY OF THE SPIRAL STAIRS

Two mysteries surround the spiral staircase in the Loretto Chapel: the identity of the builder and the physics of its construction.

The Loretto Chapel in Santa Fe, New Mexico, was built with no easy access to the choir loft, 22 feet above the main floor. Carpenters were called in to address the problem, but they each concluded that access to the loft would have to be via the ladder as a staircase would interfere with the interior space of the small chapel. The sisters (nuns) made a novena, which is a nine-day prayer.

A man and a donkey appeared after the nine-day prayer. He stepped into the chapel to say a prayer and noticed the dilemna of the sisters. He asked the nuns if he could build stairs to the choir loft. The sisters thought that he was joking, but agreed to humor him and the head nun said yes. This man went into the woods to gather the wood he needed. He steamed some to produce certain curves in the wood. Months later the elegant circular staircase was completed and the carpenter disappeared without pay or thanks. After searching for the man (an ad even ran in the local newspaper) and finding no trace of him, some concluded that he was St. Joseph himself.

The staircase carpenter, whoever he was, built a magnificent structure. The design was innovative for the time and some design considerations still perplex experts today.

SPIRAL STAIRS OF LORETTO CHAPEL

THE SPIRAL STAIRS PUZZLE

Clue 1	Action	Clue 2	Action	Answer
frighten SCARE	minus	run event RACE	=	S
a little wet DAMP	minus	very angry MAD	=	P
to catch fish BAIT	minus	night flyer BAT	=	I
chicken BIRD	minus	make an offer BID	=	R
an animal DEER (DEAR)	minus	primary color RED	=	A
pencil center LEAD	minus	summer drink ADE		L
not large SMALL	minus	place to shop MALL	=	S
to sample TASTE	minus	place to sit SEAT	=	T
end of race TAPE	minus	puppy PET	=	A
Indian head CHIEF	minus	kitchen head CHEF	=	I
to boast BRAG	minus	to carry things BAG	=	R
sharp shout SCREAM	minus	goes with ice CREAM	=	S

THE STORY OF THE TERRA COTTA FIGURES FROM XIAN, CHINA

Xian (pronounced *shee on*) was the original capitol of China. It is located in central China in the province of Shaanxi. Two thousand years ago China was made of many provinces. Each province had its own emperor; each emperor had his own laws and rules. Then there came an emperor by the name of Qin Shihuangdi. He lived about 240 B.C. This emperor united all of the emperors and their provinces into a unified China. Qin created a system of weights and measures; he also devised a monetary system for all of unified China. Qin was a great leader.

A farmer was digging a well near Xian in 1974. He suddenly struck a hard object. Experts were called in from Beijing, the present capitol of China, to identify these life-size figures. This digging is called a pit. There are five of these pits, all facing the tomb of Qin. The archeologists determined that these terra cotta figures were constructed and buried about 200 B.C. There are over 6,600 of these figures in the main pit. The pits are over 700 feet long and about 100 feet wide. They know the exact width because of the placement of some of the figures. The arms, legs, heads, and bodies are all hollow.

The figures are about 5 feet tall. This was the height of the Chinese people 2,000 years ago. The Chinese have uncovered over 8,000 of these life size figures. They also discovered some horses and carriages.

The Chinese people wanted to do something special for this emperor after he died. They wanted to build an army of soldiers, workers and tradesmen to protect and help their emperor. They built life-size figures and buried them in the ground facing the tomb of Qin. These are the figures that the farmer discovered.

They were buried under 15 feet of dirt. A trench was dug and the figures were placed in this trench. The Chinese people put heavy logs across the trench and placed a cloth material over the logs and covered everything with dirt. Eventually the logs and cloth fell apart and this all fell into the trench damaging many figures. The Chinese Government is trying to put these pieces together, like a giant jigsaw puzzle. The people doing the digging have not found two faces exactly alike.

THE TERRA COTTA PUZZLE

Clue 1	Action	Clue 2	Action	Answer
red veggie BEET	minus	honey maker BEE	=	T
frighten SCARE	minus	some families have 2 CARS	=	E
hair on face BEARD	minus	necklace part BEAD	=	R
group of soldiers ARMY	minus	mom's month MAY	=	R
VCR need TAPE	minus	a dog PET	=	A
place to sit COUCH	minus	sound of pain OUCH		C
to rot SPOIL	minus	an error SLIP	=	O
lose weight DIET	minus	to lose life DIE	=	T
it carries food TRAY	minus	sunbeam RAY	=	T
hot water STEAM	minus	flower part STEM	=	A

THE XIAN PUZZLE

Clue 1	Action	Clue 2	Action	Answer
doctor's picture X-RAY	minus	light beam RAY	=	X
winter tree PINE	minus	animal cage PEN	=	I
Texas STATE	minus	exam TEST	=	A
soup veggie BEAN	minus	picture on $5.00 ABE	=	N

TERRA COTTA FIGURES

TERRA COTTA FIGURE

A HORSE FOUND IN THE PIT

THE STORY OF THE SHOGUN PALACE

A Shogun is a very special person. He is a general in the Japanese military. He is not just any general but a very important leader. There is a Shogun Palace in Japan that has special floors. These floors squeak when a stranger comes into the palace. The people who are entitled to be in the palace walk along the walls to avoid the squeaking floors. The palace was built especially with these squeaky floors. It is a manner of alerting people in the palace that a stranger has entered.

THE SHOGUN PALACE PUZZLE

Clue 1	Action	Clue 2	Action	Answer
price COST	minus	army bed COT	=	S
60 minutes HOUR	minus	his and mine OUR	=	H
not shut OPEN	minus	writing tool PEN	=	O
rye or oat GRAIN	minus	flower need RAIN	=	G
W	minus	sheep EWE	=	U
pleasant NICE	minus	something cold ICE	=	N
fuzzy fruit PEACH	minus	for one EACH	=	P
VCR need TAPE	minus	cat PET	=	A
bottom of room FLOOR	minus	top of house ROOF	=	L
Indian boat CANOE	minus	one time ONCE	=	A
king's home CASTLE	minus	to take STEAL	=	C
frighten SCARE	minus	mark after a cut SCAR	=	E

GENERAL INTEREST

THE STORY OF SMOKEY THE BEAR

Many years ago there was a forest fire in the state of New Mexico in the Capitan Mountains. The Forest Rangers from the Nogal Ranger Station found a bear cub that survived the fire. They brought this cub to the ranger station. The author's aunt and her husband were in the station when the rangers brought in the cub. The bear's fur had absorbed a lot of smoke. The rangers began to call the cub "hot foot teddy." The author's aunt had to take care of this cub. She did not like the name "hot foot teddy." She and two other people named him "Smokey" because he smelled like smoke. The name stuck and the bear would accompany the rangers when they visited schools and fire departments to talk about fire safety. Thus, the legend of Smokey the Bear was formed.

SMOKEY THE BEAR

THE SMOKEY THE BEAR PUZZLE

Clue 1	Action	Clue 2	Action	Answer
corner sign STOP	minus	spinning toy TOP	=	S
postman brings MAIL	minus	feel poorly AIL	=	M
water vessel BOAT	minus	needed for baseball BAT	=	O
form of water LAKE	minus	ginger drink ALE	=	K
to rip TEAR	minus	black goo TAR	=	E
place to get ice cream DAIRY	minus	what we do to a refrigerator RAID	=	Y
red veggie BEET	minus	honey maker BEE	=	T
not expensive CHEAP	minus	measured step PACE	=	H
sugar tree MAPLE	minus	light source LAMP	=	E
dog's feast BONE	minus	1st in a race WON (ONE)	=	B
potatoes come from these EYES	minus	agree YES	=	E
space AREA	minus	hearing tool EAR	=	A
hair on face BEARD	minus	necklace part BEAD	=	R

THE STORY OF THE 4 STATES AND THEIR CAPITALS

There are four state capitals that have the same first letter of the name of their states. One was the first state of the Union and another was the last state entering the Union. The states and their capitals are: Dover, Delaware; Honolulu, Hawaii; Oklahoma City, Oklahoma; and Indianapolis, Indiana.

THE CAPITAL PUZZLE

Clue 1	Action	Clue 2	Action	Answer
to hurry RACE	minus	hearing tool EAR	=	C
change color PAINT	minus	1/2 quart PINT	=	A
sleeveless garment CAPE	minus	high card ACE	=	P
middle vowel			=	I
place to eat TABLE	minus	cotton measure BALE	=	T
Charles NAME	minus	adult boys MEN	=	A
animal skins PELTS	minus	dogs PETS	=	L
4th vowel	plus	4th letter	=	S

THE STORY OF LOCKS OF LOVE

It is not necessary to always give the children a challenge to make items interesting. Below is an item of interest to children because of their feelings for someone in need, such as children with cancer.

Many children that are suffering from cancer need to take very strong drugs to help cure their cancer. This medication, called chemotherapy or radiation treatments, causes the children to lose their hair. A group called "Locks for Love" gathers hair from people (it must be at least 10 inches long) and makes wigs for the children who have lost their hair.

THE STORY OF HEARING AND EXCESSIVE LOUDNESS

There is a part of the inner ear that is very important for us to understand what is being said; it is called the cochlea. The cochlea looks like a spiral seashell. There are many hair-like fibers around the spiral. These fibers separate the different frequencies that we hear. Sounds are transmitted to the brain and the brain sends a message for us to understand these sounds. (Demonstrate the different frequencies with a large rubber band).

These fibers are very sensitive to loud sounds. The louder the sound the more the fibers bend. They return to their normal position when the sound stops. Sometimes, these fibers can bend so far they do not return to their normal position. This could result in a loss of hearing. The loss of hearing could become permanent if the loud noise or music happens frequently. Therefore, it is important to turn down the volume of the radio or television to a reasonable level. Boom boxes and other loud amplifying devices will cause permanent hearing loss.

THE STAR OF BETHLEHEM STORY

Many years ago, astronomers divided the sky into 12 sections. Each section represented one very old family. There was an unusual formation of stars in a section that was denoted to the house of David. There appeared a very bright star in this area. It actually was three planets in a row. The astronomers predicted that an important event would happen in the house of David. It was predicted that there would be a king born to the house of David. They kept studying the stars for a clue to this event. Finally, there appeared in the sky a star that seemed to be brighter than normal. It actually was the planet Venus. Then an unusual event happened; Venus had been an evening star for many years and suddenly it could be seen in the morning. There were a number of stargazers from an area that is now Saudi Arabia who had seen this change in Venus. There were three men who observed this change; they were the three wise men or Magi. These three men followed this morning star until it became an evening star again. It was at this point that the star seemed to be over the town of Bethlehem.

Mary and Joseph were of the house of David and had to go to Bethlehem to register. The baby Jesus was born while they were in Bethlehem. The three wise men found the newborn king in a manger behind an inn that was already filled with other families that came to Bethlehem to register.

THE STORY OF THUNDER AND LIGHTNING

Thunder is the result of lightning hitting something. The light from lightning travels very fast. The sound of thunder travels much slower. It takes sound about five seconds to travel one mile. Therefore, when you see the lightning you count: a thousand and one, a thousand and two, a thousand and three, a thousand and four, a thousand and five; and then you hear the thunder and you realize the lightning was a mile away. Anything less than five seconds, the lightning is closer than one mile.

THE STORY OF PINE CONES

Shortly after the end of World War II, there was a man who was walking down some country roads. He carried a bag full of plastic bags and a bunch of rubber bands. This man would approach a house and ask the owner if he could put several plastic bags on the branches of the man's trees. If the owner said yes, then this gentleman would select certain trees and place a bag around one of the pine cones and fasten it with the rubber band. Then he would go further down the road and repeat the process. He recorded in his notebook when and where he had placed the plastic bags. He also indicated the type of tree. Sometime later (about one month), he returned and collected the plastic bags that were all numbered and identified. There were several pine tree seeds in each plastic bag. The seeds are inside the pinecones and when the heat from the sun hits the cones the seeds pop out. Thus, he was able to collect and identify many seeds from these different trees. He took the seeds and planted them in boxes. Later, when the sprigs were larger, he planted them in the ground. He watched over and cared for the small trees until they were sufficiently large that he could sell them. This man became the owner of one of the largest tree nurseries in the United States. It is amazing what can be reaped from a few plastic bags and some rubber bands.

PEACE SYMBOL STORY

This is another case where it is not necessary to pose a puzzling problem with the children. They are almost all familiar with this symbol. The author was a signalman during World War II. One of the systems he had to learn for communication was the semaphore flag system. This is the case where the man holds a flag in each hand. The various positions of the arms and hands signal a specific letter. The two arms extended downward at 45 degrees to the body, signifies the letter "N" and the two arms straight up and down stands for the letter "D." The peace symbol designates nuclear deterrent. Therefore, the letters N and D.

"N"

"D"

PEACE SYMBOL

APPENDIX A

CHILDREN'S COMMENTS

Date: May, 19, 2003

Dear Mr. Jagers,

Thank you very much Mr. Jagers! My favorite BLT was the Morpho Butterfly. You taught me a lot of things in all the BLT's. And thank you for coming to our classroom. I hope I see you next year

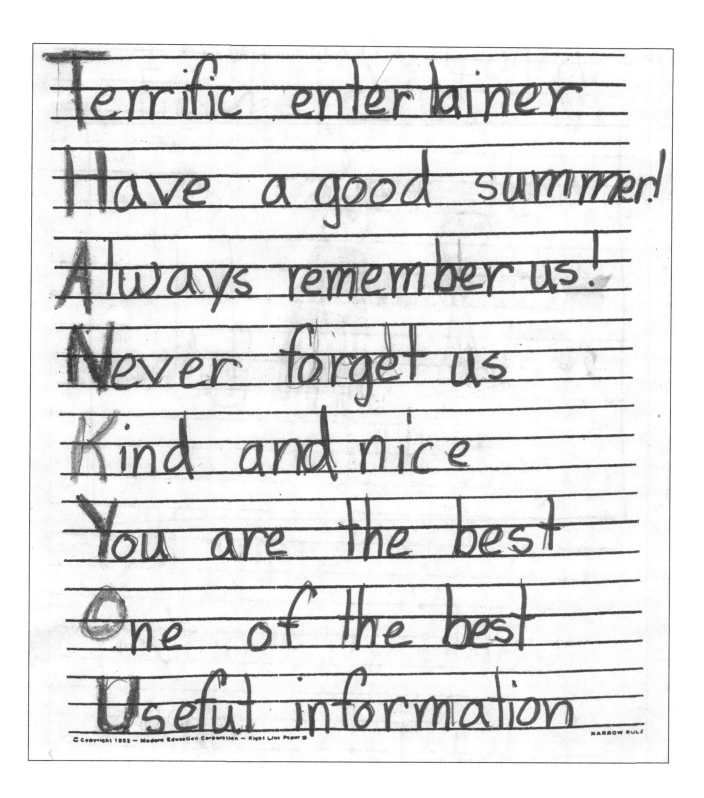

Terrific entertainer

Have a good summer!

Always remember us!

Never forget us

Kind and nice

You are the best

One of the best

Useful information

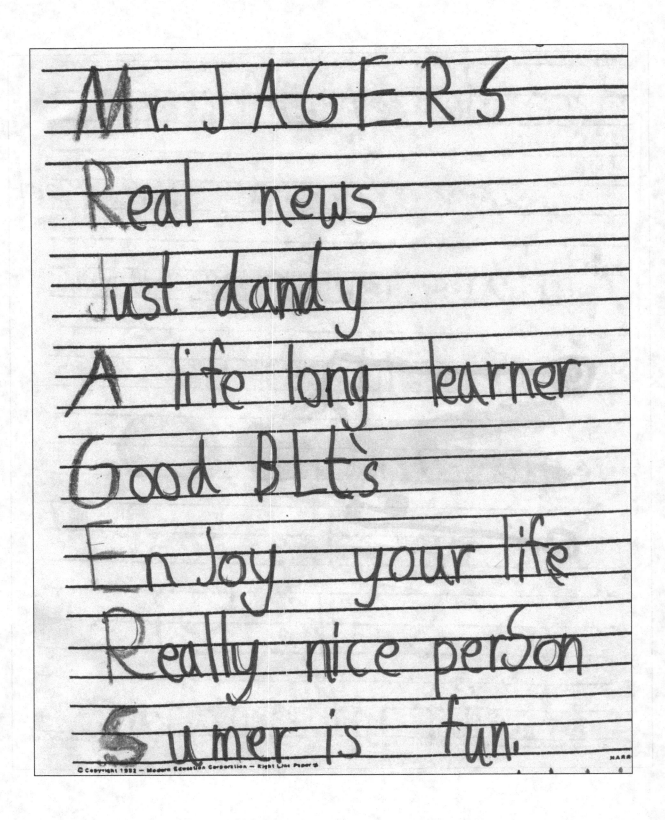

Mr. JAGERS

Real news

Just dandy

A life long learner

Good BLT's

Enjoy your life

Really nice person

Sumer is fun.

Dear Mr. Jagers,

Thank you for giving us the BLT'S it was fun how you make the hole in your hand and New birds and all you taught us was fun. I like the languages you taught us, it was so fun how we do the activities you taught us.

Dear Mr. Jagers,

Thank you for teaching us your BLT's. My favorite BLT was the Spiral Staircase. Thank you for showing us different kind of birds. And some of your BLT's on the computer Thank you for teaching us how to say hello in different Languages. I like you're BLT's and you're hints. I liked the play Mayling and Bailing. My favorite thing to down the → board was write the Letters on the board.

Dear Mr. Jagers,

June 2002

Thank you for all the things you taught me you are a very nice person. Your BLT's are very interesting. My favorite BLT was the one with the buried statues and thanks for all the languages you taught me.

.

Dear Mr. Jagers,

6/3/05

Thank you for teaching me how to do BLT's. Now I love doing BLT's with my family. Sometimes I even give my mom and dad BLT's before they go to bed. I really appreciate everything you have done in second grade for me.

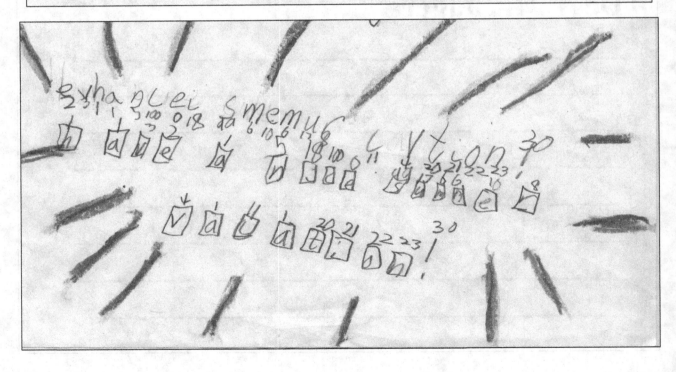

May 31, 2002

Dear Mr. Jagers,

Thank you for all your help with all of your lessons through the year. It really helped me learn cool stuff. I would go home and tell my family everything that I learned. My parents didn't even know all of the things. I am very thankful that you took your time to help me learn something new every day. Thank you.

May 31, 2002

Dear Mr. Jagers,

I've really enjoyed your BLT's. It was great learning about new and exciting things in a fun way. Thank you for making time for us. My favorite BLT's were the ones about Smokey the Bear and the bird who knew if danger was near. I'm going to miss having you because I'm going to 4th grade. I hope you miss me too.

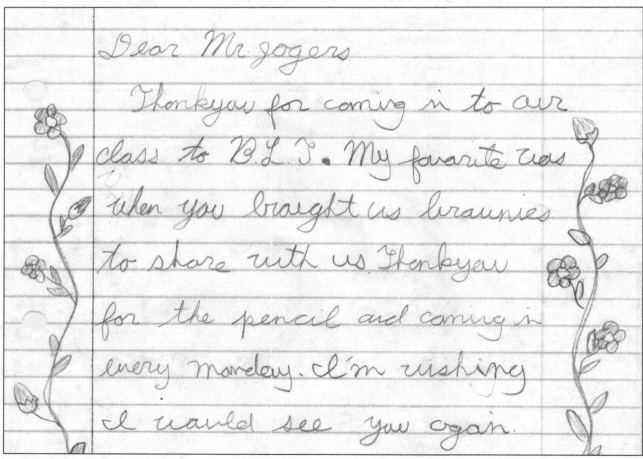

Dear Mr. Jagers

Thankyou for coming in to our class to B.L.T. My favorite was when you braght us braunies to share with us. Thankyou for the pencil and coming in every monday. I'm wishing I would see you again.

June 3, 2004

Dear Mr. Jagers,
   Thank you for spending your
time with us here at Lonicera Elem.
We enjoyed your BLT's.
My favorite one was the rainbow
one. I don't know how you did it.
I think the way you do it is like
reading it out of a book.

   I enjoyed every step of the
way. I will always think of
you.

        Have a nice summer!

Dear Mr. Jagers,

We really thank-you. It's always nice to see your cheerful face on a cold rainie day. You always cheer us up. You make our brains work right. Only you!

Dear Mr. Jagers,

Thank you for spending your time with us. We really enjoyed your B. L. T. Having you come here was a great pleasure. I hope you will come here again some day. Oh, I forgot to menshein your riddles were really good too. I have too ask you a question. Do you do B. L. T. in faarth grade? I hope so because I like those riddles and your B. L. T. Thank you again.

May 30, 2003

Dear Mr. Jagers,

I think you are very nice
AND funny. Thank you for
coming to Mrs. McCoys class
every Monday! I had fun! I
remember a time when I
was Doing the puzzle AND
you asked me, "What Does MJ STAND
for?" AND I said "Michael Jackson?"
"NO." you said. AND then you jumped
AND Nearlly touched the lights
like a basket ball Player AND I
said "WOW." then I said "Michael Jordan!"
You maDe history AND Biography
fun! I Hope you remember me!
I am not going to this school
next year. I saw you in
the memorial ParADe! Me AND
my frieND shouteD "Mr. Jagers!"
It was fun. By for Now!

APPENDIX B

WORD LIST TO PRODUCE ANY DESIRED LETTER

This list is suitable for 2nd and 3rd grade levels.

A

Acorn-Corn	Adore-Rode
Afar-Far	Afire-Fire
Aide-Die	Alone-Lone
Area-Are	Bait-Bit
Bead-Bed	Beast-Best
Canoe-Once	Chain-Chin
Chair-Rich	Diaper-Pride
Dial-Lid	Dear-Red
Grain-Grin	Lead-Led
Name-Men	Paint-Pint
Pain-Pin	Read-Red
State-Test	Steam-Stem
Tape-Pet	Area-Ear

B

Bale-Ale	Bare-Are
Bend-End	Bill-Ill
Base-Sea	Bath-Hat
Bawl-Law	Beach-Each
Bead-Ade	Bear-Are
Beard-Read	Beard-Dare
Beast-East	Beat-Tea
Beat-Eat	Beat-Ate
Beef-Fee	Belly-Yell
Belt-Let	Bend-Den
Bent-Net	Birch-Rich
Bird-Rid	Black-Lack
Blade-Lead	Blast-Last
Blink-Link	Block-Lock
Bloom-Loom	Blow-Low
Blows-Slow	Boar-Oar
Boat-Oat	Boil-Oil
Bold-Old	Bone-One
Boot-Too	Border-Order
Both-Hot	Bounce-Ounce
Bowl-Low	Bowls-Slow
Brace-Care	Brace-Race
Brag-Rag	Brain-Rain
Brake-Rake	Branch-Ranch
Bread-Read	Bread-Dare

Break-Rake   Broom-Room
Maybe-May   Table-Late
Table-Tale

C

Aces-Sea	Acids-Said
Acre-Ear	Acts-Sat
Brace-Bear	Cage-Age
Call-All	Camp-Map
Camel-Meal	Camel-Lame
Cancel-Clean	Cancel-Lance
Cant-Tan	Cape-Pea
Cape-Ape	Care-Are
Care-Ear	Cart-Art
Cart-Rat	Cart-Tar
Case-Sea	Cash-Ash
Cash-Has	Castle-Steal
Cedar-Dare	Cedar-Read
Chair-Hair	Once-One
Chill-Hill	Chip-Hip
Chop-Hop	Cider-Ride
Clamp-Lamp	Claw-Law
Clean-Lean	Clean-Lane
Clear-Real	Clip-Lip
Clock-Lock	Close-Lose
Cloud-Loud	Cold-Old
Couch-Ouch	Cover-Over
Crack-Rack	Crate-Tear
Crate-Rate	Crow-Row
Sea	

D

Aged-Age	Band-Nab
Band-Ban	Beard-Bear
Beard-Bare	Bend-Abe
Bind-Bin	Bread-Bear
Card-Car	Cedar-Race
Cedar-Care	Cider-Rice
Damp-Map	Danger-Range
Danger-Anger	Dangle-Angle
Dash-Ash	Dent-Ten

Dent-Net | Detach-Teach
Detach-Cheat | Dice-Ice
Dill-Ill | Done-One
Down-Now | Down-Won
Deeds-Seed | Dam-Ma
Dance-Cane | Dare-Are
Date-Tea | Date-Ate
Dear-Are | Dill-Ill
Driver-River | Road-Oar

G

Aged-Ade | Ages-Sea
Among-Moan | Angel-Lean
Angel-Lane | Angle-Lean
Angle-Lane | Bang-Ban
Grain-Rain | Gym-My
Page(LEAF)-Ape | Page-Ape
Page-Pea

E

Acre-Car | Adore-Road
Afire-Fair | Ages-Sag
Ages-Gas | Agree-Rage
Agree-Gear | Aisle-Sail
Ashes-Sash | Bare- Bar
Bean-Nab | Bean-Ban
Bear-Bar | Beast-Stab
Beat-Bat | Beat-Tab
Cape-Cap | Care-Car
Cereal-Clear | Deal-Lad
Dead-Add | Deer-Red
Degree-Greed | Dense-Send
Dime-Dim | Dine-Din
Easy-Say | Ewe-We
Hate-Hat | Lead-Lad
Maple-Lamp | Page-Gap
Pear-Rap | Ripe-Rip
Same-Sam | Scare-Scar
Scare-Cars | Tear-Rat
Tear-Tar

H

Aitch | Bath-Bat
Chart-Cart | Chase-Case
Cheap-Pace | Cheap-Cape
Chop-Cop | Chore-Core
Dash-Sad | Hair-Air
Hear-Are | Hear-Ear
Heat-Ate | Shift-Fits
Heat-Tea | Shore-Sore
Where-Were | Shore-Rose
I lying down

I

Afire-Fare | Afire-Fear
Aide-Ade | Aisle-Sale
Bait-Bat | Chief-Chef
Dial-Lad | Dishes-Sheds
Hi-Aitch | Pail-Lap
Pail-Pal | Pain-Pan
Pair-Rap | Pine-Pen
Praise-Pears | Rain-Ran
Raise-Ears | Raise-Ares
Tires-Rest | Wise-Sew

F

After-Tear | After-Rate
Beef-Bee | Fail-Ail
Fall-All | Fast-Sat
Fill-Ill | Flip-Lip
Flow-Low | Flower-Lower
Fog-Go | Fore-Ore
Four-Our | Fowl-Low
Deaf-Ade

J

Jams-Sam | Jaws-Was
Jaws-Saw | Jade-Ade

K

Ankle-Lean	Bake-Abe
Ankle-Lane	Brake-Bare
Bark-Bar	Break-Bare
Break-Bear	Cake-Ace
Dike-Die	Knife-Fine
Lake-Ale	Like-Lie
Rake-Ear	Rake-Are
Spike-Pies	Speak-Peas
Take-Eat	

L

Alert-Tear	Alter-Rate
Alert-Rate	Alter-Tear
Alter-Tare	April-Pair
Blade-Bead	Blast-Stab
Blank-Bank	Blink-Link
Blow-Bow	Blind-Bind
Clear-Care	Cellar-Clear
Bloom-Boom	Bowl-Bow
Clear-Race	Deal-Ade
Dill-Lid	Floor-Roof
Lead-Aid	Large-Gear
Learn-Near	Lead-Ade
Learn-Earn	Slit-Sit
Table-Beat	

M

Clamp-Clap	Cream-Race
Cream-Care	Farm-Far
Mail-Ail	Male-Ale
Mall-All	Mart-Art
Mile-Lie	Mike-Ike
Mill-Ill	More-Ore
Ramp-Rap	Team-Ate
Team-Tea	

N

Ants-Sat	Band-Bad
Barn-Bar	Bang-Bag
Bean-Abe	Bend-Bed
Bent-Bet	Cane-Ace
Bind-Bid	Clean-Lace
Cant-Act	Dine-Die
Diner-Ride	Near-Are
Near-Ear	Never-Ever
Nice-Ice	Snip-Sip

O

Adore-Dear	Adore-Dare
Adore-Read	Alone-Lean
Alone-Lane	Allow-Wall
Aanchor-Ranch	Boar-Bar
Before-4	Boat-Bat
Point-Pint	Spoil-Slip

P

Apple-Pale	April-Rail
Apple-Leap	Apple-Pail (Pale)
Cape-Ace	Carpet-Trace
Dipper-Pride	Damp-Mad
Grape-Gear	Grapes-Gears
Peach-Each	Pare (Pair)-Air
Pear (Pair)-Air	Pipe-Pie
Pint-Tin	

R

Alert-Tale	Alter-Tale
Alert-Late	Alter-Late
Arm-Ma	Army-May
Beard-Bead	Bird-Bid
Beer-Bee	Brake-Bake
Brag-Bag	Bread-Bead
Break-Beak	Care-Ace
Broom-Boom	Carve-Cave
Chore-Echo	Cider-Dice
Clear-Lace	Diner-Dine
Crow-Cow	Driver-Diver
Grape-Page	Read-Ade
Read-Aid (ADE)	Shirt-This
Tear-Ate	Tear-Tea

S

Acts-Cat	Aunts (ants)-Tan
Ants-Tan	Boost-Boot
Bowls-Bowl	Case-Ace
Cast-Cat	Dash-Had
Cost-Cot	Dense-Need
His-Hi	OTTFF__
Past-Tap	Posed-Dope
Scream-Cream	Sears-Ares
Scare-Care	Scare-Race
Seat-Ate-Tea-Eat	Shall-Hall
Slid-Lid	Slip-Lip
Small-Mall	Snip-Pin
Spill-Pill	Swear-Wear
Stop-Pot	

T

After-Fear	Beet-Bee
Beast-Base	Beat-Abe
Cant-Cat	Crate-Race
Crate-Care	Debt-Bed
Death-Head	Dent-Den
Detach-Ached	Diet-Die
Heart-Hear	Table-Bale
Seat-Sea	Eats-Sea
Thirst-Shirt	Tray-Ray

U

About-Boat	Aunts-Tans
A cup-Cap	Cause-Case
1/2 of W	W-Ewe
W-You	Wound-Down

V

Adverb-Bread	Carve-Care
Brave-Bear	Carve-Care
Cave-Ace	Dive-Die
Diver-Ride	Driver-Ride
Evil-Lie	Seven-Seen
Travel-Later	Vest-Set

Vote-Toe
Stove-Toes

Save-Sea

W

Arrow-Roar	Swear-Ears
Bawl-Lab	Sweat-Seat
Swept-Step	Swing-Sing
Wall-All	When-Hen
What-Hat	Where-Here
Will-Ill	Wish-His
Wow-Ow	

X

Exert-Tree	Exit-Tie
Exist-Ties	Extras-Tears
Six-Is	Taxes-Seat
X-rays-Rays	

Y

Belly-Bell	Diary-Raid
Daily-Laid	Daisy-Said
Delay- Lead	Easy-Sea
Hockey-Choke	May-Ma

Z

Gaze-Age	Zips-Sip
Zebra-Bear	

APPENDIX C

EXAMPLES OF THE PROBLEM CLUES UTILIZED
BY MR. JAGERS DURING HIS BLT'S

These are the actual clue problems used for the second and third grades.
The answers are in capital letters within the parenthesis.

A

Several links (CHAIN) minus part of the face (CHIN)

Many links (CHAIN) minus something below the nose (CHIN)

Oak seed (ACORN) minus a summer vegetable (CORN)

Oak seed (ACORN) minus we eat the ears (CORN)

Illinois (STATE) minus exam (TEST)

To change color (PAINT) minus 1/2 of a quart (PINT)

Beauty and the_____ (BEAST) minus tops (BEST)

To win (BEAT) minus a wager (BET)

If Z = 26 what does won =?(A)

An Indian boat (CANOE) minus one time (ONCE)

Water carrier (PAIL) minus part of the mouth (LIP)

Oat or rye (GRAIN) minus small smile (GRIN)

VCR need (TAPE) minus friendly animal (PET)

Pencil center (LEAD) minus to have been ahead (LED)

What to do to a book (READ) minus a primary color (RED)

Charles (NAME) minus adult boys (MEN)

Place to sit (CHAIR) minus have much money (RICH)

Part of a necklace (BEAD) minus place to sleep (BED)

Very hot water (STEAM) minus part of a flower (STEM)

Not hard (EASY) minus OK (YES)

B

Wind does to sails (BLOWS) minus not fast (SLOW)

Maker of honey

Hairs on face (BEARD) minus do to a book (READ)

Place to put things (TABLE) minus not on time (LATE)

Is needed to think (BRAIN) minus needed to grow flowers (RAIN)

Not sure (MAYBE) minus mom's month (MAY)

Furry animal (BEAR) minus plural of is (ARE)

C

Where to keep a laptop (CASE) minus (C) (SEA)

Animal of the desert (CAMEL) minus cooked dinner (MEAL)

Royal home (CASTLE) minus to rob (STEAL)

One hump or two humps (CAMEL) minus need a cane (LAME)

One time (ONCE) minus 1st in a race (WON)(ONE)

One time (ONCE) minus won (ONE)

Middle letter between 1st and 2nd vowel

A place to sit (COUCH) minus sound of pain (OUCH)

Atlantic ocean (SEA)

To hurry (RACE) minus hearing tool (EAR)

2ND letter before 2ND VOWEL

D

Peril (DANGER) minus certain distance (RANGE)

Apple drink (CIDER) minus Chinese food (RICE)

Place to drive (ROAD) minus boat gear (OAR)

A sour pickle (DILL) minus not feeling well (ILL)

5th letter before the 3rd vowel

One that steers (DRIVER) minus flowing water (RIVER)

E

A furry animal (BEAR) minus a metal rod (BAR)
Sugar tree (MAPLE) minus light source (LAMP)

A sheet in a book (PAGE) minus space (GAP)

Opposite of love (HATE) minus something to wear (HAT)

Sheet in a book (PAGE) minus a space between (GAP)

Ready to eat (RIPE) minus to tear (RIP)

Thin coin (DIME) minus not bright (DIM)

Bell shaped fruit (PEAR) minus musical talk (RAP)

Not hard (EASY) minus to speak (SAY)

Breakfast food (CEREAL) minus not hazy (CLEAR)

Place for ushers (AISLE) minus needed to move boat (SAIL)

4th letter before the middle vowel

Potatoes come from these (EYES) minus agree (YES)

To frighten (SCARE) minus mark left after a cut (SCAR)

F

To turn over (FLIP) minus part of the face (LIP)

3rd season (FALL) minus everything (ALL)

3rd letter before 3rd vowel

4 (FOR)(FORE) minus metal in the ground (ORE)

Cannot hear (DEAF) minus summer drink (ADE)

G

Leaf in a book (PAGE) minus a small vegetable (PEA)

Paper leaf (PAGE) minus an animal (APE)

Part of a tree in a book (LEAF) (PAGE) minus an animal of the jungle (APE)

Paper leaf (PAGE) minus an animal (APE)

2nd letter after the 2nd vowel

Part of a book (PAGE) minus a green vegetable (PEA)

A space (GAP) minus father (PA)

H

Not expensive (CHEAP) minus a step (PACE)

An eye lying down (I)
To listen (HEAR) minus R (ARE)

What ears do (HEAR) minus corn carrier (EAR)

Along the sea coast (SHORE) minus beautiful flower (ROSE)

Side of an ocean (SHORE) minus an ache (SORE)

Seaside (SHORE) minus flower (ROSE)

Along the water (SHORE) minus a flower (ROSE)

To cut vegetables (CHOP) minus policeman (COP)

A job for a child (CHORE) minus apple center (CORE)

3rd letter after the 2nd vowel

Aitch

To run after someone (CHASE) minus pop is sometimes sold by (CASE)

Head covering (HAIR) minus necessary for life (AIR)

Location question (WHERE) minus plural of was (WERE)

I

Plates (DISHES) minus loses fur (SHEDS)

Greeting (HI) minus aitch (H)

Water carrier (PAIL) minus what you lose when you stand (LAP)

Where an usher works (AISLE) minus car for————(SALE)

Cause an ouch (PAIN) minus something in the kitchen (PAN)

Parts of the car that touches the road (TIRES) minus to take it easy (REST)

Mississippi has four (I)

Need to catch fish (BAIT) minus night flyer (BAT)

Changes colors (PAINTS) minus trousers (PANTS)

Change colors (PAINTS) minus something to wear (PANTS)

To lift something (RAISE) minus corn units (EARS)

Middle vowel

Main person (CHIEF) minus main person kitchen (CHEF)

Too (TWO)(PAIR) minus talking music (RAP)

A winter tree (PINE) minus an animal cage (PEN)

J

Danger part of an alligator (JAWS) minus cutting tool (SAW)

K

To gather leaves (RAKE) minus corn measure (EAR)

Connection; leg to the foot (ANKLE) minus not fat (LEAN)

4th letter before the 4th vowel

A very large nail (SPIKE) minus some pizzas (PIES)

L

A small cut (SLIT) minus to enter a chair (SIT)

Not dim (CLEAR) minus to hurry (RACE)

Not on time (LATE) minus hot or cold drink (TEA)

Storage place (CELLAR) minus blue skies (CLEAR)

Below the 1st floor (CELLAR) minus not hazy (CLEAR)

Storage place (CELLAR) minus see through (CLEAR)

Place to eat (TABLE) minus tempo (BEAT)

3rd letter after the 3rd vowel

Pencil center (LEAD) minus to help someone (AID)(ADE)

A little fat (PLUMP) minus a way to move liquid (PUMP)

Not small (LARGE) minus anger (RAGE)

Big (LARGE) minus unit to change speed on bicycle (GEAR)

Why school (LEARN) minus not far (NEAR)

To study (LEARN) minus to merit (EARN)

Bottom of a room (FLOOR) minus top of a house (ROOF)

M

Exit from an expressway (RAMP) minus talking music (RAP)

Exit from an expressway (RAMP) minus A knock at the door (RAP)

4th letter after the middle vowel

A place to shop (MALL) minus everything (ALL)

Top of milk (CREAM) minus a running contest (RACE)

N

Pleasant (NICE) minus very cold water (ICE)

At no time (NEVER) minus at all times (EVER)

Picnic pests (ANTS) minus I formed a lap (SAT)

Walking support (CANE) minus high card (ACE)

Fingers are part of this (HAND) minus past tense of to have (HAD)

Soup vegetable (BEAN) minus picture on $5 bill (ABE)

Ring (BAND) minus not good (BAD)

A place to eat (DINER) minus what you do in a car (RIDE)

Divide the alphabet in half. What is the letter at the top of 2nd half (N)

O

Needed to hold a boat (ANCHOR) minus a place for horses (RANCH)

By ones self (ALONE) minus a pathway in the woods (LANE)

Not after (BEFORE) minus B4

To rot (SPOIL) minus an error (SLIP)

Water craft (BOAT) minus needed for baseball (BAT)

For minus 4 (O)

To permit (ALLOW) minus part of a room (WALL)

To let someone do something (ALLOW) minus room divider (WALL)

A wild pig (BOAR) minus a place to serve drinks (BAR)

P

Two of a kind (PAIR) minus necessary to breathe (AIR)

Fruit needing a shave (PEACH) minus won (ONE) (EACH)

Fruit for wine (GRAPES) minus needed to change speeds (GEARS)

5th letter before the 5th vowel

Fuzzy fruit (PEACH) minus won (EACH)

Fall fruit (APPLE) minus water carrier (PAIL)(PALE)
Rainy month (APRIL) minus train track (RAIL)

A fall fruit (APPLE) minus type of jump (LEAP)

Area (SPACE) minus high cards (ACES)

Cost (PRICE) minus Chinese food (RICE)

Red or green fruit (GRAPE) minus needed to change speeds (GEAR)

Smoking instrument (PIPE) minus a nice dessert (PIE)

A mist (SPRAY) minus sunbeams (RAYS)

1/8 of a gallon (PINT) minus a metal (TIN)

Dish (PLATE) minus not on time (LATE)

R

Necessary for a sandwich (BREAD) minus part of a necklace (BEAD)
To do to a book (READ) minus lemon drink (ADE)

Used to clean the floor (BROOM) minus loud noise (BOOM)

Sweeping tool (BROOM) minus loud noise (BOOM)

Big black bird (CROW) minus milk machine (COW)

Black bird (CROW) minus farm animal (COW)

Group of soldiers (ARMY) minus mom's month (MAY)

Stand on tiptoes (REACH) minus for one (EACH)

Rain month (APRIL) minus water carrier (PAIL)

Red or green fruit (GRAPE) minus part of a newspaper (PAGE)

Something to wear (SHIRT) minus not that but _____ (THIS)

A place to eat (DINER) minus to eat (DINE)

Person steering a car (DRIVER) minus special swimmer (DIVER)

To write clearly (PRINT) minus 1/2 of a quart (PINT)

S

Large department store (SEARS) minus R R R (ARES)

Place to sit (SEAT) minus hot drink (TEA)

Place to sit (SEAT) minus having eaten (ATE).

To frighten (SCARE) minus TLC (CARE)

A sharp yell (SCREAM) minus top of milk (CREAM)

Lady relatives (AUNTS)(ANTS) minus happens with the sun (TAN)

4th letter after the 4th vowel

An article's price (COST) minus a camp bed (COT)

Not large (SMALL) minus group of stores (MALL)

OTTFF———next letter (S) 1 2 3 4 5 (S)(SIX)

To frighten (SCARE) minus running contest (RACE)

Mississippi has 4 (S)

Winter rain (SNOW) minus at this moment (NOW)

T

To lose weight (DIET) minus to lose a life (DIE)

Body pump (HEART) minus what the ears do (HEAR)

Inside pump (HEART) minus what ears do? (HEAR)

Tempo (BEAT) minus 16th president (ABE)

Body pump (HEART) minus in this place (HERE)(HEAR)

Place to sit (SEAT) minus ocean (SEA)

In need of a drink (THIRST) minus piece of clothing (SHIRT)

Something to carry food (TRAY) minus sunbeam (RAY)

Given as a valentine (HEART) minus to listen (HEAR)

5th letter after the 4th vowel

1/2 Quart (PINT) minus sharp object (PIN)

U

W minus YOU

An item used to drink (A CUP) minus hat (CAP)

Result of a stab (WOUND) minus not up (DOWN)

1/2 of 2 female sheep (EWE)

A letter (W) minus a sheep (EWE)

1/2 of a W

V

One steering the car (DRIVER) minus one not steering the car (RIDER)

W

Yew + You +Ewe minus U

A favorite in the playground (SWING) minus what birds do (SING)

To perspire (SWEAT) minus place to sit (SEAT)

2 evergreen trees (YEW,YEW) (W)

Mothers of lambs (EWE+EWE) (W)

Cleaned with a broom (SWEPT) minus part of a stair (STEP)

Upside down mother (MOM)(WOW) minus a hurt sound (OW)

What letter asks a question (WHY) minus greeting (HI)?

X

Doctor's picture (XRAY) minus light beam (RAY)

Y

Every day (DAILY) minus to have put down (LAID)

The sport of the Stanley cup (HOCKEY) minus to gag (CHOKE)
4th letter after the last vowel

Letter that asks a question (WHY)(Y)

Z

An animal from Africa (ZEBRA) minus an animal from North America (BEAR)

5th letter after the 5th vowel

NUMBERS

1—Tone minus 20th letter (T)

4—For (4) minus none (0)

7—Sum of opposite sides of a die

9—Number for I

APPENDIX D

SOURCES OF INFORMATION AND IDEAS

National Geographic Magazine

History Channel

Animal Channel

Learning Channel

PBS Channel

Readers Digest Magazine

The Children